D0672542

Edith Ann

· ·

my life, so far

as told to and illustrated by

Jane Wagner

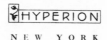

HYPERION

NEW YORK

Copyright © 1994 Jane Wagner.

All rights reserved. No part of this book may be used
or reproduced in any manner whatsoever without the
written permission of the Publisher. Printed in the
United States of America. For information address:
Hyperion, 114 Fifth Avenue, New York, New York
10011.

ISBN 0-7868-6120-7

BOOK ILLUSTRATIONS
JANE WAGNER

BOOK DESIGN /ART DIRECTION
DEBORAH ROSS

DESIGN/TYPESETTING
ROBERT VEGA

FIRST EDITION

10 9 8 7 6 5 4 3 2 1

Edith Ann

•••••••••••

my life, so far

When you are a kid,
you look at life
and you do not have
the slightest idea
what you are looking at.

Childhood comes at a time in your life when you are too young to understand what you are going through. And you're too young to understand that you are too young to understand.

Everything at this stage is just guesswork.

Dr. Lopez, my feelings doctor, hung up this poster on the wall, it says, "It's never too late to have a happy childhood." Frankly, I think your chances of having a happy childhood while you're still a kid going through it are pretty slim.

So it's a good thing you get a chance to have it later in life.

Because like the poster says, while it may not ever be too late to have a happy childhood, at my age it could be too early.

**The hardest part about being a kid
is knowing you have got your
whole life ahead of you.**

I am at that awkward age:

I am old enough, now, where I can reach more things without standing on tiptoe, but I am still young enough where they don't want me to have what I can reach.

I'm too old to believe there are monsters under the bed and too young to defend myself in case there are.

**No sooner had I learned to tell time,
than I began arriving late everywhere.**

Take it from a kid, when you drive past a school playground and see a bunch of kids laughing and giggling and swinging from the jungle gym—jumping around, playing games, blowing bubble gum, telling jokes—don't think this is what we are really like.

This is just recess.

I like short stories. I like to read them and I like to write them. They are short and to the point. They are harder to write, but worth all the work. This is one of the shortest of my short stories. It takes almost no time to read, but it took 2 days to write and could still use some work.

Once upon a time, yesterday, the beautiful Princess Edith and her dog Hug decided they would play Henny Penny and Chicken Little. Then we ran into the house and the Princess screamed, "The sky is falling. The sky is falling." And Mom said, "Edith, I am busy. Go back outside and play." Sadly, the beautiful Princess and her dog went back outside and let the sky fall down on them.

The End

I'm thinking of entering this somewhere to some magazine. Any ideas?

MORNING IN Edgetown

My mom says I have to be more positive,
and I say life has to be more positive too
or it's just not going to work.

We moved here to Edgetown, my dad said as a "stop-gap measure." When we got here, I was already potty trained. I did everything early for my age. We moved here from Bakersfield. I will always have a soft spot in my heart for that place. It is where I learned to walk and tie my shoes and dress myself. It is where I licked my first cake pan and it is where I got whooping cough and first tasted cherry-flavored Nyquil. It is where I had my first asthma attack.

Daddy was let go from his defense job where he helped make parts for top secret aircraft. Spy stuff! We moved here hoping for a better life. We still have our hopes up.

Mom says she wishes we could move, but I would hate to leave my treehouse out back.

I love my treehouse, but it has no TV and no fridge so I am in and out a lot.

I like early mornings best, before rush hour. The neighborhood is as still as a TV test pattern.

I take my diary and go out on the porch with Hug and we just enjoy the quiet. The only time in the day when the birds can hear themselves sing.

Criminals stay out most of the night and are late sleepers. So the morning is the safest time for kids like me and senior citizens who like to power walk, like Mrs. Milfred.

Sometimes she'll pass by and we'll have a nice chat. Sometimes we say nothing. We know when not to bother each other. We send out signals. Hers are real strong. It's a pretty good way to get to know somebody—then if it turns out we don't like each other—nobody has to ever know. This way no one will get their feelings hurt.

I use colored pencils to write in my diary. I write the sad parts in blue. The happy in orange. I use red when I am mad. On days when nothing happens, I put a big "zero." On days when something happens, but I am not sure what, I put a big "question mark." This way I can thumb through and see what kind of week it was without having to relive all of the details.

Has this ever happened to you?

You're coloring in your coloring book and you have a brand new piece of chewing gum in your mouth and it drops out and you don't even know it and then you get up and step on it in your socks.

Here is something adults always say
that I do not like:
"Edith, what do you want
to be when you grow up?"
As if what I am right now is not enough.

Mom and Dad always say, "Edith, just be yourself." Even though they criticize everything about me. And then when I am being myself, they say, "Stop doing that." They never seem to get what I was doing was just being myself. Either they don't know who I really am or I'm really not who they had in mind.

They did everything to get me to walk and talk. And now sometimes it feels like all they want me to do is sit down and shut up!

They just don't get it—

I wish I had a quarter every time my parents said, "Edith, you are being childish." Excuse me, but shouldn't a kid my age have the right to be childish? It's one of the few perks we have left. Not that I blame them for wanting us kids to act more like grownups. I wish my parents would act more like grownups, too. But it just does not seem to work. Acting childish seems to come naturally, but acting like an adult, no matter how old we are, just doesn't come easy to us.

Dear Senator:

I think I know how to make the world better. Here's my idea. Kids learn how to act in the world by seeing how grownups act in the world. I don't think the world can ever get better unless this changes. We must make grownups act differently. If this is not possible, then we should protect little kids from being around how grownups act. If the grownups will not cooperate, we will just have to put warning stickers on the ones who are not suitable for kids to be around.

Yours truly,

Edith
Ann.

Six is a big turning point in life. You don't want to make any mistakes. That's why you see a lot of six-year-olds behaving like they are still five.

IN the Future

Dr. Lopez, my feelings doctor, says some-times a person needs to go to a place you can't get to by traveling there. This is how she talks. This is her way of saying I need to go inside myself. It's not her way to say things in such a way that you know exactly what she means. Sometimes she likes you to be unsure about what she means. See, she knows while I'm trying to figure out what she means, I'm bound to learn something about myself. She tries to get me to search around for what she calls "pieces of the puzzle." The puzzle is me, see, and all the stuff that happens to me, well, that's what she calls the pieces. I think we may have bitten off more than we can chew. There could be some pieces missing, then what?

Has this ever happened to you? You get handed this puzzle, you open up the box and you look inside and you can just tell there are pieces miss-ing. It's not that you lost them—these pieces did not make it into the box, in the first place. Or even if the puzzle comes from the factory with no pieces missing—by the time I get around to the point where I am about halfway finished, I will start having a problem with missing pieces.

Childhood is the leading cause of stress among kids my age.

I think back on those early days when Daddy and me would just kick back and shoot the breeze—we'd talk about grownup things. We might tackle some CNN-type global issues or we'd talk about all the layoffs down at the outdoor carpeting factory, or he might just open up some beers—and we'd put in some Jim Croce tapes, sing along or just listen close to the words.

This was before we knew Daddy had a drinking problem. Daddy and I were the last to know. In fact, I don't think it was even that much of a problem to us.

Now, he's in a 12-Step Program. I'm proud of him, because I am sure he would rather be drinking.

Some kids seem to know how to
make their wishes come true.
They have a knack for it
or maybe they just know what wishes
are likely to come true and they stick with them.
It's not like they can *make* their wishes come
true, see; it's just they're more level-headed
than me at knowing what to wish *for*.

I see now there's a whole other way of wishing.

Sometimes I think it is like this:

God has a TV set
and God watches us on it.
Whenever I think I'm being watched,
I always sing and dance
and do a commercial for myself.

Baby Jesus was so lucky
when he was a kid.

He had a light on his head
so he could read comics in bed.

Here's what I don't like:

**Sunday school teachers
who give you homework.**

A teacher should know a lot of kids come from unhappy homes and giving them too much homework doesn't make their home life any happier.

I like a teacher who gives you something to take home to think about besides homework.

I sent away and got this great history of humanity wall chart and it finally came and it stretches around the whole room. I started putting it up and I stretched it out along the wall and I needed just a little bit of my sister Irene's wall to put up the whole thing. And, would you believe, she wouldn't let me use even a small piece of her side of the room and I had to tear off a big hunk of history. That's just an inkling of what I go through.

Here's what bugs me:

Parents who yell at you to stop yelling.

I'd rather Mom and Dad yell at me
than each other.
When they yell at me it's for my own good.

When they yell at each other
it does no one any good.

What about this: You have this cut on your thumb. You think it's healed. You think to yourself, "I feel like doing some finger painting." So I started painting a red brick house.

Then suddenly, you feel a sting in your thumb. I look down and see I have mixed blood from my cut into my painting! I almost threw up.

Then, Ms. Taylor, my art teacher comes by and she says, "Edith, you have outdone yourself. The red practically jumps off the page. It's vibrant, and alive." I said nothing. She gave me four stars and hung it up.

I just hope it won't form a scab.

The Band-Aid is what I call a great idea. And a household item no house should be without. I am a big customer of Band-Aids and, at least once or twice a day, in fact, I need to put one on.

If I knew who had the idea, I would write a note of thanks or maybe I would just take a plain Band-Aid and write the word, "Thanks."

I try to get as much living in as possible,
because they say childhood does not last
as long as it used to.

"Time flies
 and so
 do bullets."

Those last three lines I made
into a haiku poem
which I entered in a poetry contest.

Keep your fingers crossed.
I'll let you know if I won.

Another short story.
This may be my shortest story yet:

Once upon a time, the beautiful princess Edith got mad at the world and threw a terrible Rumplestiltskin temper tantrum. Her mother said, "Edith, you have got to control your temper!" I said, "You're my mother, can't you control it for me?"

The End.

Dr. Lopez never tries to stop me when I have one of my temper tantrums. She doesn't shoot me critical looks to shut me up. Which is one good thing since half the time it is those critical looks that get me worked up in the first place. Whatever I do, I can scream, cry or sometimes I will just clam up like a clam. She accepts it. I think she even expects it.

I can tell her the worst things about myself—things I cannot even mention here, but she is never shocked—not so far, at least. Not to my face, anyway.

She acts like she knows what I am doing and why. And it is OK. I think her plan is this: to just let me be myself until I get so fed up with being this way that, at some point, I will snap out of it and begin to change.

Dr. Lopez gave me a new power button
and when you look at it with one eye
closed, it says,

"IT WAS THE BEST OF TIMES."

and when you look at it with
your other eye closed, it says,

"IT WAS THE WORST OF TIMES."

this way, she says,
I am dressed for all occasions.

I invited Mrs. Milfred—she said I could call
her Ida—to come to my tree house for deep-
dish pizza and when I asked if I could pencil
her in, she said, "Yes." And then she did not
show. Meanwhile I had ordered the pizza and
cleaned up the tree house which was filled with
leaves because the cracked roof leaked. And I
threw some throw pillows from the living room
around.

I waited for her quite a while, then I had to
climb down the tree and go inside, find her
number and call. Her line was busy. Busy.
Busy. Then finally she answered. I told her I'd
been waiting. She said she thought I was pre-

tending. I told her if I was pretending, I would not need to pencil her in. I would just invite her up and then forget about it.

And then I just slammed the phone down and hung up on her. Then I had to call her back to say I was sorry. But her line was busy again. I kept calling. Then I got through and said I was sorry I flew off the handle. And she said she was sorry that she missed my pizza party.

Suddenly it hit me, that the pizza had not been delivered to the tree house, which I could see out the window. So, I called the pizza place to ask why the pizza never came to my tree house. And can you believe it, they thought I was pretending too. So I just slammed down the phone in disgust.

Then Hug scratched at the door to get in because it had started to rain. Then Dad came in looking for the remote control. Naturally he said he saw me with it last. But I said he had it last because I remembered seeing him tuck it inside the pocket Mom had sewed onto the throw pillow.

Then Mom came home. She asked what was

the matter? But she didn't wait for me to answer. She went in the living room then she came back in the kitchen and asked, "Where are the throw pillows?" I said nothing. Because at that point I did not feel like talking to anyone.

This afternoon when Ida didn't show and the pizza didn't come, I thought things couldn't get much worse. But I was wrong. Things were not even close to how bad they could get.

I still had to face the wet throw pillows. Especially the one with the wet remote control in the wet pocket.

There should be a 911 1/2—
an alternative 911.

Where you could call in for help and
you get to decide if it's an emergency,
not the operator.

Then they'd just have to believe it
and send help.

I don't see how my parents who don't seem to understand who I am or one single thing about me or what makes me tick, or how I feel about things, always seem to know when I am lying.

We all kind of keep to ourselves here in Edgetown, which is a good idea considering all the feuds going on. Somebody is always getting put out with something somebody said or did. I know that from my own personal run-ins with people.

A lot of hard feelings are floating around. We have people here who cheat on their spouses. Then we have a gossipy bunch that feeds on everybody's troubles. Everybody knows what everybody else is doing, and this cannot help but create some ill wills. It has started getting really bad now that so many Edgetowners are popping up on the TV talk shows and telling stuff about each other to the whole world.

Daddy says we have got one of everything here in Edgetown. Mom says that's an understatement! We have got a bunch of serious skinheads here. Just two blocks away, down by the Grab 'n' Go, is a storefront where they hand out their hate stuff. They like to sign up young kids, but so far they have left me alone. Knock on wood.

Daddy says he is sure if there was a contest for what town has supplied more kooks for the talk shows, Edgetown would win hands down. I know for a fact, people from Geraldo's show keep their eyes peeled on us here, knowing what a bunch of hotheads we are. How else can you explain why we have been seeing so many people from Edgetown on TV, making fools of themselves. I heard, last week, somebody was here snooping around from the Montel Williams show.

Oh, it is no worse than most places, I guess. It is no more awful here than, oh let's say, Bakersfield, or New York or L.A. It is just a typical American town. That is the good news and that is the bad news, as my sister, Irene says.

And wouldn't you know, of all the skinheads there are in this country, Geraldo would have to zero in on our local bunch here and invite them on his TV show to have a showdown with a group of gays. The gays were also from Edgetown. They came on to tell the skinheads they were not going to stand for their gay bashing threats which, of course, was exactly the wrong thing to say and seemed to just pave the way for more threats.

The fur started to fly. Daddy and me watched the whole awful thing. Geraldo kept saying that the skinheads came from a growing organization based in Edgetown. He must have said "Edgetown" a good eight or nine times. I don't ever remember him making such a point of what place a group came from. It will just make the skinhead problem we have here worse. Now that they got so much free publicity.

Geraldo made sure things got out of hand, because they like to get people fired up. It makes good TV. It is all about ratings. Daddy said he wished someone would break Geraldo's nose again. The big shock though was seeing Ms. Taylor up there (with the other gays) speaking out about gay rights—not that there was anything new about that—no, she had outed herself about 5 weeks ago to the school board and everybody else in Edgetown.

So we all knew what she had to say about

gay rights—for 5 weeks she had gone on about that to everyone. But to see her do this on network TV, well I'll admit it was a shock to hear this skinhead call my teacher a "dipstick dyke"—she took offense to the word "dipstick," but used the word "dyke" herself several times.

Daddy said she showed a lapse in good judgment. I think he meant her going on Geraldo—not her being gay.

I clipped this out of *USA Today* and put it on my sister's pillow:

Lab rats that listen to hard rock only live 18 months and rats that listen to soft candlelight music live 40 months.

My sister Irene's days are numbered.

I heard on the evening news that working at a convenience store is one of the most dangerous jobs in America. They didn't say anything about the dangers of shopping there. Of course, this is a five-part news feature.

It's a trick they do to hook you into watching their news—when they get a juicy feature about something they know you'll want to watch, they tease you with little bits at a time.

What usually happens is they get you to watch for those extra details you need to know—only by then you forget what you were watching for and it goes right in and out of your head.

Wait and see, after watching all five parts all I'll know is how dangerous it is working at convenience stores, which was the very first part. This is always the way.

I am a steady customer at the Grab 'n' Go, see, it is a part of my life. I cannot stop going there just because it's dangerous. It is too convenient. Too convenient for armed robbers, too. Ha-ha.

This is just about the only feature they've ever done that I felt could really help me—but it would have helped more if I could have learned it all in that first part. But *no*, they have to stretch it out and by Thursday I could go to the store for some bread and maybe get caught in a holdup and end up dead. Because maybe what could have helped me avoid getting bumped off was held back to be shown on the last segment. And for what? Ratings!

They tell me I have got a mind of my own, but sometimes it's like my mind itself has its own mind. Things happen inside my brain that I know nothing about—like, what makes something suddenly pop into your mind, I wonder? Like you can be eating lunch and you suddenly think of something that has nothing to do with what you are having for lunch.

One minute you may be enjoying a peanut butter and banana sandwich. The next minute your mind wanders and before you know it, the bell rings. Lunch is over, and the whole sandwich is gone but all you remember enjoying is those first two bites. The milk is gone too but the only proof that I drank it is if I am left with a milk mustache.

Mom says the mind works in mysterious ways. I think the mind is even more mysterious when it is not working. I guess you could say the same about your heart.

I was watching Daddy shave the other morning. I wonder why the hair on your face that you don't want keeps growing back and the hair on your head that you do want keeps falling out?

I love riddles.
I love to read them.
I love to think them up
and think them out.
Here is one I just thought up
and cannot figure out:
How come the real riddles in life
do not ever get into the riddle book?

I used to think learning something meant having the right answers. Some grown-ups, see, they want us kids to come up with answers to their questions. But, Dr. Lopez wants me to come up with my own questions.

And it's her job to help me come up with the answers. I must say this comes as a welcome change. After all, we're not dealing with a subject like math here, we're dealing with a real live person, a card-carrying member of the human species, as my sister would say. I could be a boon to society or a big blow to it. Right now I'm a toss-up.

Let's hope for all our sakes Dr. Lopez knows what she's doing.

**Growing up
can take
a lifetime.**

For a while we were hoping we could get a Hard Rock Cafe to open up here in Edgetown. But they did a study and turns out a lot of our teenagers when they reach a certain age just pick up and run away. Usually to big cities where they already have a Hard Rock Cafe. So there are not enough teens here to support a place like that. All we have left are some grunged-out slackers. Mostly Butthead and Beavis couch potato types. There's something about Edgetown that rubs teenagers the wrong way. It's been a local trend now for quite some time. They reach a certain age—they're outta here. My sister's just turned that age and I cannot wait till she runs away. And not just because I could then have the bedroom to myself. But because I think it would be best for everyone concerned.

She is a born misfit. She doesn't belong in Edgetown or in school. She doesn't belong on planet earth. It's like living with this dark cloud under the same roof. She makes herself and everyone around her miserable. I have to walk on eggs and even then she still flares up. I'm trying not to let her warped view of life rub off on me. She's been a real disappointment to Mom and Daddy. Which is what I hate. The last thing they need is more disappointments.

In a few years, I will have to take biology
and the teacher will expect us to dissect a frog
which I have already decided I will not do!
I care more about what frogs *feel* like inside
than what they *look* like.
A frog (until someone dissects it)
is one of the few living creatures
that really seems to enjoy life.
They invented the game of leap frog.
And they play it better than anyone.
This is everything we need to know about frogs.
Although of course there is much much
more to know.

There are two main types of teachers:
Teachers who call on you when they think
you know the answer. And teachers who call
on you when they're pretty sure you don't.

Some teachers look at you and make you feel
like you can do no wrong. Some look at you
and you feel like you can do nothing right.

You can learn from both types—
but you learn totally different things—
about them and yourself.

Here's what really bugs me:

Teachers who give assignments like,
WHAT I DID ON MY SUMMER VACATION

What if you didn't have a vacation? What if you
had a lemonade stand and worked all summer
and what if you only made four bucks and some
change and the lemons and sugar and cardboard
for the stand cost much more than you made.
Plus $2.60 for a broken punch bowl. Would I
want to write about this horrible experience?
I don't think so.

You know what happens
when you get angry?

First, your face gets just like a fist.
Then your heart gets like a bunch of
bees that flies up and stings your brain
in the front. Your eyes are like two dark
clouds looking for trouble. Your blood
is like a tornado. And then you have
bad weather inside your body.

Irene says no one in the family understands her. It's like we're all living an alternative life-style.

Hey, maybe, that's what childhood is—an alternative life-style.

"Alternative." I always learn lots of good words from Irene. I pick up a lot of stuff from her. Good and bad. After all, she is my big sister so I'm sort of forced to have her as a role model. She has a pretty good vocabulary—but I bet she can't spell most of the words she uses.

She's got a short attention span, plus being dyslexic, plus she's dropped out of school. Yes, she's got the whole family worried. That's how I think she likes the family to be.

I have never thought of myself as coming from a happy home, but sometimes when I have been away and the car turns and I look down the block and I see my house, I feel so happy to be home.

That's something. That's really quite a lot!

You know what?

We have a lot of crime in Edgetown so we started up a neighborhood watch program and crime <u>has</u> gone down since we've been watching our neighbors.

You know what else?

We're pretty sure my friend Jill's dad used
to sell drugs. But we didn't tell the cops
because sometimes they tear down
the wrong house.

**Parental guidance sounds good, but,
without knowing the parents,
it means nothing.**

JUST THINK:

**every single person on planet earth
had to be potty trained.**

There's a certain night that keeps popping up in my head. It was still light out and I was sitting on the porch steps fiddling with a knee scab that wasn't ready to come off but was coming off anyway because I scraped my knee again and opened up the same spot for the second time.

Daddy was on the porch sitting in one of those aluminum lawn chairs, sipping some beers from a can. His brother, Uncle Claude, was here visiting for a few days—stopped by on his way back from the state pen where he saw Stanley. Stanley's the youngest of the Bewley brothers and he is doing time for a crime he says he did not do.

I am not sure what the crime was—nobody is talking, but we are pretty sure he did it—given his past and all. Mom says all three of the Bewley boys have a wild streak—Stanley's got the wildest. I think I have got a pretty wild one myself.

Anyway, about Uncle Claude, he really does have a drinking problem and wouldn't you know he's about the only man around who's not a 12-stepper. All day, everyone had been dropping hints that he should get help. But he said he was too far gone as a die-hard drunk and the thought of a lifetime being sober seemed far more depressing than a lifetime being loaded.

Then Daddy said, "Claude's the type if he ever gets into a 12-step program first thing he'll do is look around for the nearest elevator."

That got a few weak laughs which died down too quick. It got real quiet. Just in time for us all to hear Uncle Claude pouring himself a stiff one into a big iced-tea glass with just one ice cube.

Uncle Claude saw everyone eyeballing him and just guzzled it right down. He did not care. Well, he did and he didn't. You know how that is.

Mom asked if we thought the dip could use more salsa—so we all had to test the dip, of course, and we agreed it did need something. Claude's girlfriend, Bev, asked Mom if she'd ever tried Paul Newman's, and they must have talked a good ten minutes about how good

Paul's products are. Bev went into detail about his salad dressings. We're not crazy about Bev, she has a known drug problem. We think she may not be the best person for Claude. Mom says Bev's family probably feels the same about him. Of course, Bev says she is in recovery, but everybody says that.

She is one of those motor mouths—does a lot of talking without saying much. At one point, Daddy finally snapped, "Somebody put the salsa in the damn dip or shut up about it." Bev and Mom got quiet. They had been enjoying their talk, I guess. Then they went into the kitchen.

I stayed on the porch with Daddy and Uncle Claude, because I don't like salsa, no matter whose it is. All of a sudden, Uncle Claude looked at me, and blurted out, "Life is about choices, Edith. Don't think you have to turn out like them and you don't have to turn out like me, God knows. You can choose something else.

"Don't ever think you're stuck, OK? I'm stuck. I've made so many bad choices that at this point any choice I make will most likely be wrong. But you, Edith, no one at your age has to be stuck. 'Choices,' Edith, you remember that. You can make something of yourself, if you just don't get stuck."

I remember every word that was said that night. It felt like I was one of the grownups.

Some nights stick out in your mind. Maybe somebody threw a party or it was Halloween or something special like that. Or maybe there's a holdup at the Grab 'n' Go or a skinhead flare-up or a drive-by.

And some nights just stick out on their own—for no real reason exactly. It's not like anything really bad or good happened that night that should make it stick out, but it sticks out anyway, like I say, on its own.

I come from a very critical family. We are not only critical of each other but we are critical of ourselves and anyone else who happens to be around. You'd think that with all of us pointing out each other's faults all the time, we'd show some improvement.

But I think we've gotten worse. I think I should point this out to everyone that our worst fault is we are all too critical.

When my sister Irene says
"Who made this mess?"
she's talking about a few things
of mine that have somehow landed on
her side of the room.

When Mom says
"Who made such a mess of things?"
she's talking about any place
in the house where I've been
for at least 10 minutes.

When Dad says
"Who made this mess?"
he means the garage.

But when I say
"Who made such a mess of things?"
I'm talking about the world!

*I wrote this composition in English class and got a
B+. My teacher said I would have made an A
but the page was a bit too messy.*

My Child
a
Wanted Child
Planned Parenthood

Dear Mr. Limbaugh,

This letter is for my dad—even though I'm the one writing, I'm writing for him not myself. I wish you could know my dad. You two would really hit it off.

He is a good man in every way. He is a big fan of yours. And if you ever run for office he'll sure work to get out the vote here in Edgetown.

He has been down in the dumps lately over, oh, a lot of things. Most of them have nothing to do with the Democrats. I won't go into the details.

Anyway, he needs cheering up—but nothing we do here seems to work. Hearing from you would give him a real lift, I just know it. Something personal is what I want—not the usual dittohead mugs and stuff that *every* dittohead has. We already have that junk.

I'm asking for something special just for him. Maybe a golf ball with your photo. Maybe something you've worn, an old food-stained tie even. Or maybe an empty iced tea Snapple bottle autographed "To Dirk—A Great Guy And Friend."

Or, if you'd like to call—there's a card inside with our number. Feel free to call anytime, day or night. He looks forward to your newsletters and if by some miracle, as he read it through he happened to see a personal note to him, maybe a Father's Day message on Father's Day—well I can just see his face light up.

Oh, I'm sending this photo along. This is when he was working on that stealth bomber, which of course, you can't see. Ha-ha. You can keep this photo since we have other copies. When this was taken he had more hair. Now he has less hair and what he has is going grey fast. Please do something to help him snap out of it. He had some bad setbacks lately. I wish something nice could happen to him for a change.

As for me, I'm hoping you have a change of heart. You could keep your mind pretty much the way it is. It's mainly just a change of heart you need. I wish you could know me and my dog, Hug. I think we could win you over to the cause of Animal Rights. Or at least we could get you to use nicer bumper music.

Well, gotta go now.

Edith
the ECO-FREAK

Vote for KIDS '92

a tiny speck in a ruthless universe

EarthSave
Healthy People
Healthy Planet

The way I see it—the world is in a mess.
Why can't I accept that?

My room is in a mess and I've learned to
live with that.

I'm getting along pretty good now with my feelings doctor Dr. Lopez. Oh, she's far from perfect. I don't look for perfection, in fact I find it unpleasant to be around. She's so different. Most grownups—they just want kids to be good and to do what they say. But Dr. Lopez just wants me to be myself—so "good" is something that hardly ever comes up. We're trying to uncover the real me. Yes.

Okay, I admit half the time I don't know what she's doing. But I know she's doing it for my own good. That's something. It's really what you want from the grownups in your life.

Then when they make a mistake in taking care of you it helps to know they didn't do it on purpose.

I think family planning should include everyone in the family. Maybe the kids like me, who already live here would just as soon not have to deal with another kid in the house. A new baby means a big life-style change. A life-style we were maybe just finally getting used to.

Once a week my grandmom takes my baby brother to the nursing home. The old people like to pass the baby around—for some reason, that seems to cheer them up.

My grandmom loves to spoil me.
Frankly, I think she should be more strict,
but she just cannot say "no" to me.
So I have to be careful what I ask for
to protect us all.

I have been helping Dad and Claude with this new song they've been working on. All the Bewleys are natural-born musicians. All of them can play guitar by ear.

Once I choose which instrument I want to play, I will probably be able to play it by ear, too. We don't need any more guitar players in the family—so I'm looking for something else to take up.

Daddy says Claude is the one with the talent. It's true, Claude can practically do magic tricks with his guitar. I've seen him hold a guitar pick between his teeth and peck at the strings with his face, in a style unique to him. He may look kind of goofy doing it, but the music he makes is just unbelievably great!

Daddy says Claude could have been a Country and Western star if only he had tried harder. Well it can't be easy making music holding a guitar pick tightly between your teeth plucking away on those strings—each note just perfect. Oh, did I mention his guitar has twelve strings? Anybody who gets this good at something has tried very hard all right.

We never did finish the song. It was one of those, "I-feel-like-a-bug-on-the-windshield-of-life" songs and we all got too depressed when it hit us we'd been working all day rewriting a song that had been done only about a hundred times before by others.

So, to cheer us up, Claude did his guitar mouth medley ending up with this great old Porter Waggoner song, "The Rubber Room." It's about this man in the looney bin and I can't explain it—you have to hear it. A classic.

Then I started singing, "If I Could Put Time in a Bottle," thinking they'd join in, but then Mom called us in to see Vic do "Patty Cake, Patty Cake." So we gathered up the glasses and dried up bean dip and went in to watch Vic do his latest thing. It's such a duddy thing to do, really. But we make it out to be something so great, he must think he's conquered the world. He squealed so loud my ears hurt. It's the grownups I like to watch. They are so funny trying so hard to get Vic to do this really baby routine.

Then Claude started in trying to teach Vic "The Itsy, Bitsy Spider," but Vic was not up to doing his hands like a spider. I felt jealous, I'll admit. See, Claude had taught me this song when we lived back in Bakersfield. I moved over to where I made sure I could catch his eye. Then he said, "Edith, listen to these lyrics. This is a song about a spider. Not just any spider, but about a spider with spirit. It's a song about survival—a song about life." We did it together, not Vic of course, but Claude and me.

Claude and me together, singing:

> *The itsy, bitsy spider*
> *climbed up the water well,*
> *then came the rain*
> *and down the spider fell,*
> *out came the sun*
> *and dried up all the rain,*
> *and the itsy, bitsy spider*
> *climbed up the spout again.*

This is a song Claude does when he gets booked to do kids' birthdays and stuff. What I like about Uncle Claude is he isn't satisfied just to be entertaining. He wants to make us feel for the spider. I used to hate spiders. It was the one bug that really gave me the creeps. That song made me see spiders in a whole new way. I still don't like being alone with one in my room, maybe crawling on my bedspread on a damp day, but now I respect them. I can feel for them now even though I am still pretty much afraid of them.

When I look back over my life, I think of all the happy times I've spent doing things I'll soon be too old to ever do again. Like this one time I remember—I made this great sawdust puppet— Ms. Taylor was big on art projects that were supposed to teach us some important lesson about life. I think the point of this lesson was to prove that art can be anything. Something like that.

We'd all get so involved in finishing the project itself that most times she'd forget to point out the lesson of it, or maybe she did point it out and it went over our heads.

This one time, she got it into her head for us to make some puppets—out of sawdust. She'd asked us to all bring in three empty toilet paper tubes and three long-necked soda bottles. She was always asking us to bring in stuff. I don't think she had any idea of the trouble she put us to.

"Tomorrow," she'd say, "I want you all to bring in some old string and old newspaper and empty glue jars." It never dawned on her that some of our parents are not string-savers. And who keeps their empty glue jars? I've never seen an empty glue jar myself. In our house, the jar is finally thrown away not because all the glue is gone, but because it's just too dried up to be used.

And the three empty toilet paper tubes. You might find one lying around if you're lucky, but three? I don't think so. Still, how could we complain? After all, these projects took a lot of work on her part. While we were looking for string and empty toilet paper tubes, she was down at the lumber yard scooping up saw-dust which we'd later mix with wallpaper paste for our puppets. For all I know she had to run all the way over to the wallpaper store for the paste.

So, we'd bring in whatever she wanted because she was the kind of teacher who made you want to work for her. We felt if she asked us to do something, somehow it must be for our own good.

We figured she was worth the effort. I don't know why we like to please some teachers, and other teachers we could care less if they're pleased or not.

I think for one thing, with Ms. Taylor, it was maybe because we felt we could please her. Some teachers you can't please, no matter what. But Ms. Taylor was quick to flash us a smile to show us when she was pleased. Oh, don't worry, she didn't go around smiling at every little thing.

Some teachers are overly friendly just because they need to be liked. They might smile at you just to win you over or as a way of tricking you into doing something. There's a lot of mind tricks that go on around here. The teachers have their set of tricks and we students have ours.

But Ms. Taylor never needed to use mind tricks. She could get us to do anything and she was totally up front about it.

She used art, string and sawdust.

Has this ever happened to you?

You go over to the window to sharpen your pencil and something you see out the window grabs your mind and your entire pencil gets eaten up by the sharpener.

Then your teacher accuses you of not paying attention and, if you say, "How come I heard you say I wasn't paying attention if I wasn't paying attention?" She tells you "Don't talk back to me," instead of seeing that you had a good point.

Has this ever happened to you?

You fly off the handle and say things to people, especially your best friends, without thinking of the really bad effect it will have when your birthday rolls around. But I guess that is part of being human.

If you are a human being, you might as well face it: You are going to rub a lot of people the wrong way.

The other day, I was arguing with Hubby Matthews. All of a sudden, he started yelling, told me I was too bossy.
I am not bossy; my ideas are just better.

Mom says, "When your friends hurt your feelings, and say they do not want you to be the boss, you should say, 'Okay, then what do you want me to be?'"

But I cannot.
That just would not be me.

I wish my sister Irene could be like all the other teenagers in Edgetown and just run away.

One time, I had a big fight with all my friends. So I decided I was gonna get all new ones and break up with the old ones. So I did break up with them the whole grabby, geeky, buglike bunch. I thought by now I'd have new friends, but it's hard to find refills.

Right now I am angry with so many people I cannot even remember who to say hello to and who to frown at.

And what really bugs me is no one seems to care.

When a person could care less whether you are mad at them or not it is a big waste of time to stay mad.

Has this ever happened to you?

You throw away your old pair of shoes because you're sick of looking at them every day, but then you wish you still had them, because there was something about them that fit right and nothing else feels quite as good?

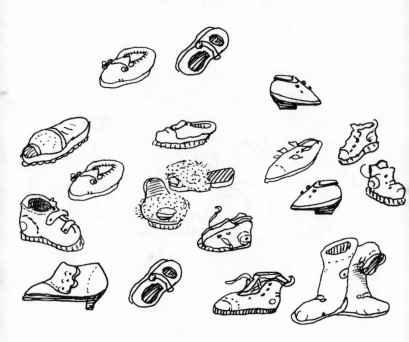

Dr. Lopez says,
we learn from our mistakes—
yeah, for one thing, we learn
how many mistakes we make.

What I'd like to learn, now,
is how to avoid those mistakes
in the first place.

**Unless you are at a picnic,
life is no picnic.**

Dear Edith,

You've said many times in your column, "Life In The Little Lane," that you are no expert. My question is why don't you give the column over to someone who is? We kids out here need help. But not from amateurs like you!

—An ex-reader, Patti

Dear Readers,

I decided to publish this letter not because I like insulting letters but to show you what I have to put up with writing this column.

—Edith

Dear Jill,

Just a note to say "Hello." We are all sorry about your dad's run in with the law. Even if he was guilty, I am sure he was not guilty of much. He was just trying to be a good provider. Dad says, these days, more and more people are forced to bend the law just to make ends meet.

I think of you, now, as my best friend. I just wish I had thought of this when you were here. I could have been nicer to you.

I hope you are not going to be ashamed to come back for a visit to see us, sometime. This could have happened to any one of our dads. We are all glad to learn that he was just selling Chinese herbs, steroids and smart pills—deprenyl and stuff.

Frankly, we thought it was much worse.

I will not go into what is happening at school. It is all bad. Dr. Lopez may be leaving. Cutbacks! What else is new? So if it makes you feel any better, my life is falling apart, too. If she goes, I go. I plan to leave with her.

Me and a bunch of other kids we are going to start a protest. We are flooding the school board with letters. They're running scared.

Hub has lost some weight—all in his face though. Everywhere else, he is the same old Hubtub we know and love. He is going away to a camp for diabetics this summer. He has to be excused two or three times, during class, to pee. Guess you heard, we lost Ms. Taylor.

Miss ya.

Edith

P.S. Do you still have your sawdust puppet?

I spent a month thinking that maybe for my birthday I'd get this new doll, Pam Glam. She really, really has it all. She's famous, she's beautiful, she has her own TV commercials. She's got jewels, a wet bar, a walk-in shoe closet, a house with a gym and attack dogs, a salad shooter, credit cards, airline tickets to everywhere. A laptop computer, monogrammed spa clothes, a Water Pik.

My birthday came, and I did not get her, and at first I was sorry but now I am sort of glad. She is living in a dream world and I sure would hate to be there when she woke up and found herself in my room.

My doll is not a real person.
And, yet, she is not a phony either.
She is just what she is: a doll.

This is both her strong point and her
weak point.

Things I like about my doll:

She never surprises me.
I can always count on her.
She is more dependable than people.
She doesn't suddenly get mad at you, and give
you critical looks.
She seems to like me the way I am which I
cannot say about anyone else in my life who
knows me as well as she does.

I am more myself with her than with anyone
else. Maybe because with anyone else when I
am myself, the critical looks start. It never
fails. No one likes critical looks, yet we all get
them and we all give them.

Of course, my doll can be boring—like all dolls (after a while, they all seem to repeat themselves). But she never makes me feel that I am boring. She is always there for me even though, at times, I forget where I last put her.

I will always take care of her, however, so that she will never have to know that we have nothing in common anymore.

I must be growing up.
I've stopped liking to play with dolls.
At a certain point, I realized that I was
giving more to the relationship
than I was getting back.

After looking everywhere—high and low—I asked Mom if she thought somehow my sawdust puppet maybe got sold at our last garage sale, and she said she didn't know, and asked me what it looked like.

Now, how can you answer a question like that? There's no way to explain what one looks like, but you should know if you've seen one.

That sawdust puppet meant something to me. I don't know what but there's a reason why I get these sudden urges for it. It was a link to something. What, I don't know. I'll never know if I don't find it. It was a part of me that I didn't want to lose. Now, of course, wouldn't you know, it's lost.

It's a nutty thing to do with your day—making a sawdust puppet. I doubt I'll ever do it again—now that Ms. Taylor has left. For one thing, who else could we depend on to bring in all that sawdust? She knew where to go for the wallpaper paste. And she wasn't afraid of the mess we would make—but now she's gone.

So that part of my life is over. The sawdust puppet part. And those three toilet paper tubes I've been saving—might as well throw them away. Without Ms. Taylor I'm never gonna make anything with them. I don't have the skill or the will.

I might as well face it, I doubt I'll ever lay eyes on Ms. Taylor again. Unless, of course, she has another lapse in judgment and shows up on Geraldo again defending gay rights to a bunch of skinheads.

Sometimes I look at Uncle Claude and there's a feeling that comes up—like those times when you feel sad, but you're not quite sure why—and if somebody should ask you why you're sad you wouldn't know what to tell them.

I don't know why I get these blue moods around him because no one can make me laugh like he can.

When he hauls off into this song and dance routine of this great tune, "The Rubber Room" about this guy who's locked up in a padded cell in this loony bin . . . but I told you about this before didn't I? You should hunt through the bins at your record store. You'll thank me. It's a song for the funny bone, not the ears.

Anyway, Claude does it even better than the record. He gets hired for parties and club dates sometimes. I bet this routine has them rolling in the aisles. I love this song the most, and the part where he does those guitar licks with his mouth, it's like a miracle how he does it. The rest of the family hates when he does this. They look at him like he's making a fool out of himself. They don't seem to get that part of what's so great is seeing someone make a fool out of himself so full out.

You have to admire someone who, first of all, gets the crazy idea to put a guitar pick in his mouth and start picking, then to stick to this idea until he got good at it. It takes willpower and talent to work all those hours practicing to get good at something that would never ever occur to most people even to get good at.

I think we should applaud Uncle Claude's talent, not shoot him all those critical looks. I'm pretty sure I've figured out why the rest of the family hate this routine most of all. It's because he has to get himself juiced up to do it. The drunker he is, the better he does it. So the family sees this routine different from me. They're thinking about how drunk he is—I'm thinking about how great he's playing. I'm not saying they're wrong. But then, neither am I.

One time Hubby got mad
and called me "No Neck."
I did not talk to him for a long time.

But then I thought,
"Why quibble over the truth?
Life, like my neck,
is too short."

I don't know what I will do if money dries up and we lose Dr. Lopez. She has made such a difference in my life. She took the kid I was yesterday and made me into the person I am today. She says not to give her the credit. The kid I was yesterday wouldn't.

She turned me onto the idea that people should try to make a difference in the world. But, as usual, she didn't stop there. She said the best way to make a difference in the world was to first make a difference in ourselves. To do that I knew I was going to have to do things a lot different and be a lot different. Sometimes just knowing where to start helps.

Although I'm full of ideas I would never have had this one on my own. See, I had it all turned around before, I thought it was up to the world to make a difference in me. This idea will help me to—as Dr. Lopez puts it—get in touch with my power.

To be honest, so far I can't say it's worked. But just the idea that I may actually have some power to get in touch with is a real surprise to me. Just the idea is something. It's really quite a lot.

At the supermarket, with Mom, I used to pretend I was lost just so I could hear them call my name over the loud-speaker.

I cannot believe how immature I used to be.

You know what, if you stare at something long enough sometimes you can forget what you're staring at. Try it.

What you're staring at starts to look less like it did than when you first started looking at it. *Yes.*

You might think at first my eyes must be playing tricks on me. But it's not your eyes playing the trick. It's your mind. *Yes.* Just more proof that your mind has a mind of its own.

You know how sometimes you can feel real smart and other times you feel really stupid? That's because you've got one mind telling you you're smart and one saying you're stupid.

Did I tell you about the time I put that Parcheesi dice up my nose? And it didn't come back for almost 2 days. It was one mind that told me to try it. "Look at that tiny little dice, so cute. Wonder if it's small enough to stick up your nose?" And so I tried it, see, and the minute I did, my other mind said, "How could you be so stupid to stick a Parcheesi dice up your nose?" We are like innocent bystanders to our own brains.

Kids do things that make their parents crazy. And parents do things that make their kids crazy. And this can be happening in a perfectly normal family. In other words, everyone in the family can be going crazy, but the family itself can be perfectly normal. That's how crazy things are.

This is to give you an idea of the kind of thing I might talk about with Dr. Lopez. It's sort of like going to a class only instead of learning about subjects like math and history, Dr. Lopez teaches me about me. I'm the subject. Crazy, huh?

One thing, I'm never bored.

Dr. Lopez says family fights can be harder on the members of the family who are not fighting than on the ones doing the fighting. In our family we all do the fighting.

That way I guess it's easier on us all.

I asked her to explain what "Family Unit" meant—something that pops up a lot in magazines I read. I had tried looking it up, but my dictionary doesn't even explain the word "family" good. Family Unit is not even mentioned. She tried to explain but, frankly, she didn't seem to be exactly sure, herself. Sometimes, I forget she does not know everything.

She says she is not Super Doc, after all. I should not think she's perfect, but it's hard not to because this is how she comes off. Most of the time, she is perfection itself.

I have read this on a shirt and it sounds true:
"Society deserves the kids it gets,"
but I have never seen
a T-shirt that said
what the kids did to deserve what we got.

You can make a difference in the world or your neighborhood. It's a great feeling. I know what it's like to be one of the ones to make a difference. The frustrating part is getting people to see the difference and proving it was me who made it.

Either I'm not making a big enough difference or somebody else is getting all the credit.

Dear Richard Simmons:

My friend Hubby Matthews, a diabetic, has a weight problem that I wish you would help him with. You have such a great personality. You could reach him and put him on a healthy diet. For a year now, he's been yo-yoing.

If you could drop by his house and go through the fridge, like I've seen you do on Sally's show—and Maury's too, I think—this could turn him around. Here's his address and telephone number, mine too. I'll be waiting to hear from you. Keep up the good work.

Edith

P.S. I wish you'd make up with Howard. I know you love his kids and life is too short.

My feelings doctor, Dr. Lopez, is the only person who doesn't try to stop me from crying. During our times together. I'll be talking and sometimes I'll be hit by a sudden mood swing and I just start sobbing—for no reason the tears start to flow. It's like my eyeballs have gone white-water rafting. Dr. Lopez will say, "It's OK Edith, just go ahead and cry."

Mom thinks mood swings come from too much caffeine, but I am pretty sure mine come from life.

The man on TV said that humankind is over 3 point 7 million years old. When I think of all I have gone through in my short life, frankly, I do not know how humankind has stood it—just think, all those billions and billions of mood swings.

I told Mom and Daddy that I was pretty sure it was not good for me to be around Irene so much, and that I had proof she was a bad influence on me. And they just looked at each other as if to say—she's not good for us to be around either, but we're stuck.

A husband and wife can get divorced, but other members of your family, like Irene, we can't unload.

And I asked Mom if she thought when I was grown I could sue my sister for damages and I asked her if she wanted to see the evidence I had against her.

She said no she did not have a legal mind but I should save it so I could show it to a lawyer someday. So this whole thing with Irene could end up in court.

Mom says in this family we don't listen
to each other enough. I think I know why:
TOO MANY TIMES WHEN WE LISTENED
WE GOT OUR FEELINGS HURT.

I think what we need to do is listen more
to what we are saying to each other.
I will make a stab at this
and I will find out what I am saying
that has made everyone stop wanting
to listen to me.

JUST THINK
Your family are the people most likely
to give you the flu.

A confession from my past:

My baby brother Vic has a soft spot on his head and Mom said not to touch it. So I took a laundry marker and made an "x" so I wouldn't forget. I'm old enough now to know better. Mom said I was old enough to know better then. But I guess she was wrong. One look at Vic's head proves that. Besides me, only a few people know, for sure, I did it—Mom, Dad, Irene and my grandparents.

Vic has no clue that I made the mark. He hasn't got a clue that he even has the mark. Anyway, we're pretty sure he'll grow out of it. If by some fluke he doesn't, well, I figure soon he'll have a full head of hair, so he could go through life and never guess he has a big laundry mark on the top of his head.

Of course if he should ever, at some point, go bald, well, he's in for a big shock. But by then it's not likely he'll blame me for it and, by then, it may look more like a mole than a laundry mark. Don't you think? I'm just going to have to try and put this behind me or I'll go stark raving nuts.

I overheard Daddy and Uncle Claude—out back sitting on the steps. Usually they like being on the front porch where there's room for me to go out and just sit around with them.

I was in the kitchen but I was close enough where I could hear them through the screen door. Uncle Claude said he's changed plans and was leaving that night, ". . . didn't want to out-wear his welcome," he said.

Yeah, right, as if he ever felt really welcome except for me and Daddy. This gave my heart a sinking feeling. I always hate to see him go. When he's here, he adds so much life to my life.

Then they switched to talk about Stanley. Then got off on their money problem stuff. I was glad when I heard Hug at the front door scratching to get in, so I didn't have to stay and listen.

Daddy and Uncle Claude can be so much fun when we're singing and making music but sometimes when they're talking about every-day things—oh, like money problems lets say— they can be just as boring as any other grownups.

Quality time is my favorite time of day.

**But with my busy schedule,
it's hard to find time for it.**

Quality time can be having a walk with Hug in the early morning when it feels safe to be out. It can be going down to Radio Shack to look around with just my dad and no one else. Or it can be hanging out with my mom at the kitchen table over a cup of coffee, talking and laughing like two adults.

Any time I spend with Mom now that she's working and the baby is here feels like quality time to me.

Dr. Lopez told me to write this down:

Every moment is a moment
that has a chance of becoming
one of those moments we will
never want to forget.

This is the way she talks. She expects
me to know what this means. I read it,
now, and I wonder if I wrote it down
right.

I used to try to make something special out of everyday. But I found it was taking up too much of my day. So, Dr. Lopez told me to try something:

Now I just try to be there when something special happens. But I don't push myself anymore to make it happen. I see now everyday is in itself special. In other words, I don't have to "make" it special, it is already special on its own—just because it is another day. I don't have to do anything but notice this. I think this is what Dr. Lopez was getting at, but don't quote me.

It's like being a couch potato only you're not watching TV. No popcorn, no earphones, no tapes. You can listen to what's there at that moment to be heard—light rain drizzling, a car driving past, a splash sound, a bird chirp.

Way down the block, a garage door opens, closes, gets stuck closing, a dog barks at the stuck door. Another bird. (A thrush, I think, this time—definitely not the one I heard before.)

Then, a few doors down, a van pulls to a stop. The motor dies—doors open and close, open and close, open—and—close. A flapping sound—maybe an umbrella opening up, more bird sounds, not singing—flying sounds—just a lot of movement (maybe looking for a drier nest).

Believe it or not, this feels great.

Mom's putting in a lot of overtime at the airport these days. We're all glad for the work, but there's just no time for her to make me a costume this year for the ecology pageant. So I've decided to send a note saying I was an endangered species that died out the night before the pageant. This way I can get out of going. I will not win, but at least no one will know I didn't have a costume.

I wonder what ants think about ant farms? Do they feel like actors or farmers? Or prisoners?
I hope they feel like ants.

Do they hate us for taking away their privacy or are they grateful to have a roof over their heads?

Do they feel they live on a nice block?

Are they really all that busy or are they just trying to make us think they are?

Do they even know they are working on a farm?

Dear Edith:

I know you're no expert, but do you know why your mind wanders?

Love,
Puzzled

Dear Puzzled:

The mind gets tired of having to come up with thoughts all the time and so it wanders off to get peace of mind. So it can have a 5-minute coffee break and come back fresh and alert ready to take more of all that stuff your brain drums up.

Edith Ann

I thought this answer was a good one, but there is a lot on this topic I don't get. How can your mind just wander off on its own—with no warning, no "excuse me please, do you mind if I wander?" Does your mind have its own mind? Does your mind make plans to go away from the constant stress of having to wait around till you make up your mind about something?

What's it thinking about when you're not thinking about anything? When you draw a blank and can't remember something, is it your mind's fault? And when you suddenly can recall something you'd forgotten, what's going on inside your brain?

Is forgetting something a relief to the mind? Is it like your memory is taking a vacation or something?

Am I using my brain or is my brain using me?

Where does a new thought come from?

When you want to forget something that happened why can't you just forget it? What is it that won't let you forget?

Your mind will help you make up a lie—then turns right around and makes you feel guilty that you lied.

When you tell yourself, "it's all in your mind," you're telling it all to your mind.

Who else is even listening when we talk to ourselves? We don't have to talk out loud. Does that mean the brain has its own ears?

When you have a closed mind, is it your mind doing the opening and closing or is it the total you?

Why does your brain help you figure out certain things—but on other things may just add to the confusion?

When I say, "What am I thinking?" what do I mean by that and why should I even have to ask these questions about my own mind?

When I understand something, did I just use my brain to help me understand this something or is my brain just making me think I understand?

Why is it so often I don't know what I'm going to think of next? Why don't I know? If our hearts behaved this way, we'd all be dead as doornails.

I know from TV what your brain looks like when it's hooked on drugs. Wonder what your brain looks like when it's hooked on phonics?

Sometimes in the bathtub, I play swimmer. And then, sometimes, I like to sit on the drain when the water runs out.

I think it feels interesting.

If they had a contest for America's worst sister, Irene would be a sure winner. We have nothing whatsoever in common except that we live under the same roof.

She makes it a point to do everything she can to push your buttons. Now she has gone too far. Body piercing and tattoos, that's her new way to get at us. I saw her Friday at that new tattoo parlor that opened up.

Dad told her he didn't want her coming home covered from head to foot with tattoos or brass bangles dangling from her nose and lips. She said she was just helping them set things up and as a trade off they were going to let her hang out and watch because she thinks she might like to be a tattoo artist as a backup to her career in the music biz.

Right now, see, she's in this grunge band "The Dyslexics" formed by a bunch of high school dropouts. A better name would be Grungee Thumpers, which describes perfectly how they look and sound. If they think they are ever going to get a record deal they are really living in some kind of dream world. If you ask me.

I am so lucky to have someone like Dr. Lopez to talk to—

Today I learned that you do not have to be afraid of the self doubts you have about yourself. They are not facts. They are just thoughts and like most thoughts can be ignored or forgotten.

Self doubts are no more real than those times when you feel self-confident. It's all in your mind. And we can change what's in our minds. I change my mind all the time, don't you?

Sometimes you need to make up your mind about something and other times you need to change it.

It sounds easy till you try to do it.

You will never believe what happened.

Remember that wish I made, that Irene would run away? Well, guess what—my wish came true. She's run away. This is the first wish I've ever had come true. Now we have one less impossible person in the house to deal with. Who knew I could do it.

I just hope she won't get homesick like I did when I was away at camp. I hope she's not too old to get her picture on a milk carton. I wish my wish had not come true.

**Nothing makes you realize
you don't know what you want more
than getting what you want.**

There comes a time when you go out to the playground and look around and it feels like a place you've never been to—or a place you can never go back to or a place you cannot stand to be in one more minute.

We went by that new tattoo parlor place to ask if they had any idea where Irene had run off to. I got to go along with Daddy since it was my idea to go there in the first place. I wish I could give you some idea of how weird-looking this place was. They said last time they saw her she was in the middle of getting a tattoo on her left butt. I shot Daddy a look on that line knowing it wouldn't sit well.

The tall guy with the red beard said he was tattooing an eye for Irene—it was going to be a big eye with long eyelashes, then he was to add the letters RENE. He said he had just made the outline of the eye and had put three eyelashes on the upper lid and that she stopped him before he was able to finish the pupil part.

He said she was a real wimp about the needle jabs—screamed bloody murder. He'd barely got started before she made him stop. Said she didn't care how empty it looked. Right here is when Daddy asked him, in a mean way too, did he use disposable needles, and they said, well of course and acted like they were insulted to be asked such a question which I don't blame them for because Daddy was shooting them some of the worst critical looks I've ever seen him shoot. It was like he'd all of a sudden grown thicker eyebrows so he could make a meaner frown.

I bet the tattooing did hurt extra bad because her butt is so boney. She's totally fat-free back there. Everywhere else too. Then the other guy came in from the back and said he saw this old road kill of a car pull up out front, honk for her and she just split. Then the one with the red beard said he got a quick look at who was in the car and the one in back looked to him like he was huffer-happy. Dad looked at me. I looked at him. No doubt we were both drawing a blank on that term. A new trend term I guess. But we weren't going to give them the satisfaction of asking them to explain something we probably should've known, so we let it slide.

Then Daddy started poking around. The place was a pig sty not even fit for a pig. I thought Daddy was smart to ask them if they disposed of their needles. I just hope he wasn't dumb enough to believe them when they said yes. One look told you these guys did not dispose of anything much.

To say these guys were string-savers would not be saying nearly enough. Let's just say they'd be more than ready for any art project Ms. Taylor could ever think up in her wildest dreams.

So, no, it wasn't likely these guys were going to throw away their old needles, if only for the reason they knew they'd never be able to find any new ones they had laying around. That's my take on it.

It was pretty clear these guys didn't care much one way or the other if we found Irene or not. So we just left. Dad didn't thank them for their help because they didn't help that much. He was pretty rude, which is how he can be sometimes.

At the door, to make up for Daddy, I waved good-bye and told them to let me know if and when they ever had a garage sale—because it looked like they had some unusual collectibles. I had spotted two lava lamps in the back. The bare-chested one wearing the vest waved back, which I thought was nice and frankly hadn't expected.

I couldn't wait to go to school Monday, I knew I had a really good story to tell about this weird place, the tattoo parlor/pig sty and the co-weirdos who do the tattoos, which, when you think of it is no more weird than our big factory here where we make outdoor carpeting for the whole world, practically.

Dear Joan Rivers,

I am writing you this letter in the hopes that you will read it. It's a long story I'll try to make short—here goes.

My mom works hard as a security guard over at the airport here in Edgetown. Last week she stopped someone, a big body builder type coming off a private plane—it was just a hunch she had—but she thought maybe in that duffle bag he had slung over his shoulder there could be some illegal steroids. So she took it on herself to risk getting hurt and bumped into him and caused him to trip in such a way that she was able to separate him from his duffle bag.

Anyway, I don't know how it all went down exactly, but turns out she had caught her a drug-dealing crook alright. Only it wasn't illegal steroids. It was cocaine he had, and guess what? He was using your jewelry to hide the cocaine in. I don't know if your jewelry is already hollowed out or if he made the hole himself. But he somehow had hidden quite a lot of the stuff.

Mom said when she first looked in she thought, "Oh this guy must be one of Joanie's jewelry salesmen." But then, because she had a pretty good knowledge of your jewelry, something made her reach in and snap open one of your flexible band bracelets with the memory wire and sure enough—tucked inside was some cocaine. And there was over 85 pieces of your jewelry.

We figured his plan was to sell the coke, then sell the jewelry too, which was in our minds a double crime against you.

So anyway I thought you'd be happy to know my mom stopped your beautiful jewelry from being used to commit a crime.

If you feel like dropping her a thank-you note it sure would be a nice surprise. We're hoping she'll get a citation maybe—but a note from you would really mean the world to her.

If you could just thank her for her bravery and how you know how hard it is to juggle career and motherhood.

Something, by the way, we have all admired you for. You could give her the lift she needs.

She and my dad have been down in the dumps. We have one of those runaway teen situations in the family. You can put yourself in my mom's place I know—even though Melissa never ran away at that age.

I've been looking for ways to cheer them up. I'm counting on your note to help cheer up Mom. For Dad, I'm hoping I can get Rush Limbaugh to do something since Dad is a real mega dittohead.

Well, thanks. Any effort on your part will go a long way. Love to you and your beautiful, talented daughter, Melissa, who I read somewhere loves horses. Me, too.

Love ya,

Edith

P.S. Do you know Rush Limbaugh? Also, I know how much you love dogs. Here's a photo of my dog, Hug. Cute, huh?

Something great happened today!

My brother took his first step. Yes! I use the word step, not steps here because he took one step, then fell, kerplunk, right down. Hard, like they fall in cartoons. It looked like he tripped over the main foot he had used to make his first step. I guess because he wasn't used to it being there.

Even though it must have hurt he didn't cry when he fell.

He was too happy to cry. He squealed so loud, Hug's ears went flat. Daddy dived over to him and swooped him up in his arms. I think Mom squealed too. Maybe I even squealed. It felt like I did.

This was a happy, happy morning. Maybe one of the best mornings we've ever had in our whole lives.

This is what they mean, I bet, when they talk about family values. This was a valuable moment for the whole family—at least the three of us who were there at that moment. I asked Mom if she was as happy when I took my first step, and she said, "Of course."

It was nice to hear that I could make her that happy. I just wish I could remember how I did it. Vic, I guess, won't remember this time either. Funny you can play such a big part in something and everybody remembers but you.

I'll be able to tell Vic about this day. I'll memorize everything about it since we couldn't get it all on video—because Irene took the camcorder with her when she ran away. Did I tell you that?

Well anyhow, we had a good celebration. A Vic for victory party. We nuked up some Sarah Lee coffee cake which I washed down with my very own cup of coffee—dark the way I like it. Seeing my baby brother take his first step made me feel more grown up somehow.

I felt proud too. I had a new feeling or something in my heart about Vic. I tell you there's something about seeing someone take their first step—it makes you see that person in a new way. For weeks he'd been trying to walk—as if he had somewhere he had to get to. He fell over and over till he was black and blue. I bet his little baby body ached all over. But he would not give up. He fought for that step. It was like he knew it was his first step. There, in that little blob of a baby brain something lit up. He knew.

And I told myself I was going to try to be a good sister to him, and somehow I'd make up for that big black "x" mark on his head. Maybe we could be close—at least closer than I am to my big sister. For one thing we wouldn't be sharing our room, which for Irene and me was the final nail in the coffin.

Yes, today was a mood swing to remember. It was the first time I ever felt in the mood to be a big sister. I always called him my baby brother. That's how we talked about him.

But, it's not how I felt about him. It was a way to explain why he was in my life. I knew

I had a baby brother, see, but until today I didn't know how it feels to have one.

I see now. Mom and Daddy have been trying to teach me that I should love my brother but I guess this was something I had to learn from him.

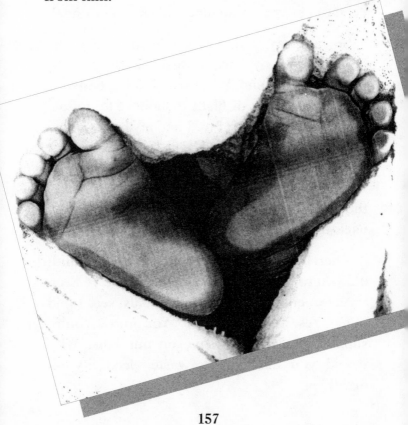

The other night I was just about to drop off to sleep, and all of a sudden I sat up in bed. And Hug sat up too. Then I got up and felt my way to the door.

It was pitch dark, Irene had taken the nite lite with her when she ran away and we've all been too busy to remember to get a new one.

So, anyway, I tiptoed down the stairs and here's the funny part, I wasn't even thinking where I was going. What was I doing tiptoeing around that time of night, I thought to myself, was I sleep walking? No, I had my hands down at my sides. They would have been straight out in front if I'd been sleep walking. Then I went over and turned on the porch light. I blinked at the light. I thought I saw something so I ran back up to bed, my heart pounding.

Then the next morning Daddy yelled, "Edith did you turn on that porch light?" We've been trying to cut down on our light bills, see. I told him, "Yes." And he said, "You know you're supposed to help us save on our bills. Why would you deliberately waste electricity all night?"

And I said nothing because I frankly didn't know what made me turn it on. Sometimes I don't know where my mind is.

Well, I might not know where my mind is— but at least Dr. Lopez does. And you know what? She figured out it's one of those things you do without thinking. This will surprise you. I turned the porch light on for Irene. This is how crazy everything is. I don't know how many times I wished for Irene to just run away. I even used up all three of my birthday wishes. But now that she's run away—I'm wishing for her to come back. I have been more unhappy with her gone than when she was here.

Dr. Lopez says leaving the porch light on can be a loving thing to do for someone. Can you believe it? Me, doing something loving for Irene? Dr. Lopez sees this as a sign I'm getting better. I think I'm acting more crazy than ever. In fact, I'm worried Dr. Lopez and me, both, have gone stark raving nuts.

It's clear we're going to have to do some more legwork to track down Irene. But we're scoping in on her. Here's what we uncovered so far. We went by this new hair place—it used to be "Sally's Savoir Hair Salon."

But a hairdresser from New York City bought Sally out and redid the place over into a His 'n Her more "happening" type hair place, "The Split Trends" for the younger set. If all the Edgetown teenagers would pop in to get their hair styled just once before they ran away—he'd make a mint!

Oh, did I tell you this place was one of Irene's "fave" hang outs. "Fave" is Irene's word for favorite. "My Fave Food . . . My Fave Crave, My Fave Bod, My Fave Hunk, My Fave Celeb, My Fave Vid, My Fave Flick . . . Fave, Fave, Fave, Fave!" She had a Fave everything.

Odd when you think how negative she is. She is the most cross, sourpuss, critical, grinch-hearted person who ever walked the face of the earth.

Anyhow why we went there was to check out any clues we could find about where Irene might've run off to. We found out enough to narrow it down to two places—Seattle or New York City.

Some think because Seattle has a big grunge music scene going, she might've gone there. But, I don't think so. She hates competition. My hunch is that she's off in New York City somewhere. I have some leads to follow through on, because the cops here, they wouldn't know grunge from Blue Grass.

We'll be the ones to find her, not the cops, because we know her habits. Besides Irene would be really p.o.'d if she thinks we sicked the cops on her.

Oh, I left out the most important part, just as Daddy and me started to leave, my mind caught onto this song playing over their speaker system—which I bet cost a bundle. The music had been blaring when we came in—Daddy asked at the top of his lungs for them to turn it down and the one with the New York City attitude did so—but with an attitude.

But now I asked him to turn it up and he said it was one of Irene's tapes, a demo. So we sat down in some great chairs and listened to the song which later I found a tape of going through one of her drawers. Here's the words:

My sister is like a visitor
from outer space
how we treat each other
is an absolute disgrace

We're not at all alike
'cept we have the same face
and we happen to live
in the very same place

How this happened to me
is still a mystery
I'm just a normal member
of the human race
but my sister is a visitor
from outer space

We have nothing in common
except the phenomenon
of being two leaves

on the same family tree
not a place either one of us
wanted to be

Some nights I look over
see her tucked in her bed
if we could start over
I'd take back some things I've said
to my sister from outer space
the stranger who somehow has my face
and her things strewn
all over the place

On the way to the car, I was thinking about how I used to watch movies with Irene. I thought about that great deathbed scene from *Planet of the Apes*. Irene was a nut about those movies, but that scene was her favorite. She'd say, "There's so much love between these two apes, you forget that it's Roddy and Kim. Watch this—look how Roddy looks at her—even with the monkey gear, you can see this deep love—"

I wonder what made her stop doing stuff like that with me?

Dr. Lopez said Irene must've been in a lot of pain. That's why she ran away. I always thought she did what she did to cause pain to us, not because she was in pain herself. But, Dr. Lopez said, no, running away was her way to cry for help. That's just like her—to run away as a cry for help. Only how can we help when we don't know where she's gone to. She is impossible to deal with.

One good piece of news though—Dr. Lopez is staying on at least through next semester. Word is she agreed to take a cut in salary. Anyway, something's being worked out for the next few months.

I feel bad that she'll have less take-home pay. I know she wants to stay on partly because of me. She would miss our talks as much as I would. In her mind, our friendship is worth a slight cut in salary.

She wants the best for me and she knows I could go into a big backslide with her gone.

I asked her one time, I said, "Dr. Lopez,

don't you ever get bored with me?" and she said, "How could anyone ever get bored with you, Edith, you have led such an amazing life!" (Her exact words).

Right here, I thought of asking her, if that was true, how come I find myself so boring? But I let it go. She seemed in such an upbeat mood, I thought why spoil it.

I want to get her something nice for Christmas.

Dear Howard Stern:

You may be wondering why I am writing so I will get right to my point. We have a runaway teenager in our family and we are trying to track her down and, if we can, bring her back home. But, first, we still have to track her down. This is where you come in.

She left with a co-runaway (much older though) who worked at this new hair place and had joined Irene's grunge band, "The Dyslex-ics." Since this person is from New York City, we think they both may have headed up there. She goes by the name, Claire-All, not my sister, the older one, the hairdresser.

My sister's name is Irene. I was going to send an ID photo, but I ran out. But here's a clip-ping about her, but don't go by the photo there, because since she's with Claire, the hairdresser, it is very likely they both have a whole new look. They are both into their hair and do each others nails and hair a lot while they write songs too, and stuff.

So, anyway, we heard Claire's older sister sometimes used to go out with Stuttering John (who works on your show). So, it may be a long shot, but she might drop by your show one morning. Not Claire's sister—I mean Claire and Irene (my sister).

We finally got your show here in Edgetown. So I listen now, Daddy too, in case Irene and Claire drop by maybe to get you to play their demo or just to meet you guys. We got your show about 8 weeks before she left—she got your book and a New Year's video tape which Mama threw out. You know mothers.

But I should get back to my point which is, if Irene should by some fluke come by, please I beg you don't play that butt bongo game with her. At least over the air, don't. It would drive Daddy back to drinking. But, if by some other fluke, you two do get into this, please be on the lookout for a half-drawn tattoo on her, I believe left butt was what the man with the red beard said.

She has the outline of an Eye there, but no pupil or iris, see, so you can't miss it. So if you start to play butt bongo and you see that Eye staring out at you with a blank stare—please I beg you, Mr. Stern, to pull her panties up quick and please, please send her back home to us.

Or, if she won't go, have Gary, Fa-Fa-Fooey or Scott or someone there call this number and hold her there or trail her back to where she's staying.

We figure they must be at Claire's sister's place which we can't find because "All" is not her sister's last name, of course. It's what Claire calls herself professionally and without a last name, she is hard to track down.

Torky used to tape your shows before school, then play them back at recess, but he got caught. They made him hand over the tapes. This school is like living in a police state.

Here's a clip from the column I write, "Life In The Little Lane"—think you might find some tidbits for your show. You don't need to pay me, you can use anything. I would like credit though, and a plug for the column and my school, which is a very good one. Not at all what you'd expect in a place like Edgetown.

You may have heard of Edgetown. Our name gets mentioned a lot on game shows where they often give runners-up prizes of outdoor carpeting we make here, "The Outdoor Carpeting Capital of the World."

You've probably heard, "And to the lucky runner-up goes four rolls of the finest outdoor carpeting ever made. For your patio pleasure, "Dura-Turf," a subsidiary of Terra Firma, Inc."

I hope you and Alice never break up. Tell her my mom thinks she must be a saint.

Oh, say Hi to Stuttering John. No, I should say, "Say H—H—Hu—Hu—Hi." I stuttered once for about 3 weeks then all of a sudden I stopped and now I'm told I have unusual verbal skills—which you may not be able to tell from this quick-written letter.

Good luck with your FCC problem. We must protect the First Amendment as they say (all the others, too). Even Mom says you should have the freedom to be disgusting because if they take away that right, what will go next? Daddy said she was being sarcastic—but who knows?

Well, hope we'll hear from you soon. Love to your three darling darling daughters and tell Robin she has a beautiful laugh.

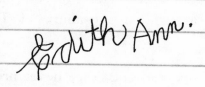

What happened next was a big blow. I don't even want to get into it. But Dr. Lopez says I must face things, not bury them. She said that what you try to bury just ends up burying you.

When I first started seeing her, she used to say I was in a state of denial. I don't see how I could have been in that state since back then I had never even heard of the word. But, since I looked up the word, well, yes, I will admit, it does seem to be a state I am drawn to. She gave me a "T for Therapy" T-shirt: "Denial is not a river in Egypt," which I never wore.

I knew it was one of those T-shirts that, if you wore it, people would just pester you to death about why you were wearing it—what's it supposed to mean and all? Like that time she gave me this T-shirt that said, "Carpe Diem"— and all day long I got pestered with questions, "What does it mean, how do you pronounce it? Is it French or Spanish? What kind of message is that to be wearing?" None of these could I answer.

I felt like a fool. I made a wild guess and blurted out "It means fish of the day." Then I really felt stupid. Frankly, I think there are times when being in that state is about the safest place maybe you can be. It wasn't until I took off the T-shirt that night that I learned what it meant. It was right there on the back all the time, "Seize the Day."

Anyway the blow that came was about Uncle Claude. Yeah. This woman called from a Ramada Inn, somewhere outside Eureka to give us the news. She sent clippings about it. They came the next day. Seems like he was booked that weekend as an opening act for some Cosmic Cowboy type, out from Austin, who must have been part of the music scene back there, but I sure never heard of him. Daddy, neither. And we both used to watch Austin City Limits, too.

Daddy put her on the speaker and the nice woman read us the clippings:

...rites
...apart in
...ns of the prob-
...g common action
...is almost impossible.
...ia Williams, a suburban
Please see REALITY, A16

...nationwide search for a ...
general manager to replac...
Waters, who retired earlier ...
year.

Wiordal went to great lengths to
praise both men and assure that
the change is not a demotion for
Please see SHAKE-UP, A22

EUREKA—The Newly Renovated Ramada Inn, located next to the Andy Divine Big Boys Clothing Outpost, closed early Saturday night due to an unfortunate occurrence resulting in an accidental death on stage at the new Old West Sidekick Lounge.

According to reports, it happened as onlookers were enjoying the "Beyond barnyard/bizarre" talents of a Bakersfield born C&W novelty performer, Claude Bewley, who was doing a "Sons-of-the-Pioneers" parody, the classic, "Clear Water."

A shocked onlooker reports: "You know that old Sons-of-the-Pioneers standby 'Clear Water'? Well, when he grabbed at his throat and called, 'Water, water' we thought of course he was just doing the song—it was only after he had choked to death that we realized he had been choking to death and was really calling for water."

It is being called death by strangulation. The speculation being that the now deceased performer somehow swallowed a guitar pick he had in his mouth, and it must have gone down the wrong way.

Yeah, sure, like there's a right way
to swallow a guitar pick.

I'll never forget that phone call. The woman who made the call went out of her way to be kind. Not because she had to. She didn't have to. She just took it on herself to do something that somebody had to do. She didn't know us and she didn't know Claude except she was there in the lounge so she got to see him do his act. Well, the first part, anyway, "The Sons of the Pioneers" parody. I wonder what makes some people be kind—just out of the blue, that way.

I watched Daddy hang up the phone. He leaned back against the kitchen counter and stood there. Mama came in from putting Vic to bed. From the look on her face she must've overheard. She had Dad's sweater draped over her shoulders like a cape. We knew what had to be done next. We had to tell Grandad and Grandmom.

Dad made the call, but Mama crossed over and took the phone from him. She gave them the news so Daddy wouldn't have to. Mama was so soft that night. Yet, strong, too. Soft, strong, not strong, strong. When she hung up, she reached for Daddy and put her arms around him. She just held him for a long while. Then she motioned for me to come over close. Somehow we worked it out so the three of us could hold each other.

Parents, when they want to be, even critical ones, can be so comforting. It's not like you have to do much to comfort someone—sometimes there's nothing anyone can do. What is comforting is knowing you have someone in your life who wants to comfort you. Last Tuesday Dr. Lopez had me look up the word "comfort." But there is a world of difference between looking it up and living it out. It almost makes you lose respect for the dictionary. Last week it was just a word I might use and this week it's a feeling I am feeling. I felt like I was in a movie where, in one scene, you are a kid and in the next scene you're a grown up.

Here, I thought of a time—I forget when—sometime after we had moved here to Edgetown. And it was way after bedtime. I should have been asleep, but I had been reading this book about the beginning of humanity and it was so totally thrilling, I couldn't get sleepy. Then I heard footsteps tiptoeing. I quickly pulled up the covers, acted like I had fallen asleep with the light on. I fluttered my eyes and saw Mom reach over and turn off the light.

Then I felt her there at the side of the bed, looking down at me. I must have looked so sweet. I had on a clean pajama top, and Mom leaned over and gave me a most beautiful kiss. It is one I will never forget. It was not like a goodnight kiss when you kiss out of habit, or a hello/goodbye kiss. It was just a kiss she gave me out of the blue for no reason other than, at that moment, she had a need to kiss me—for herself—not to comfort me, but to comfort her.

I did not see then what I see now. Children can give comfort to their parents.

I remember most of the next day being a blur. Daddy was waiting for us in the living room, dressed and shaved. He must have splashed or spilled some extra Brut. You could smell Brut everywhere. Why it was Brut I don't know, since I always give him Old Spice. I give him Old Spice, because that's what Grandad uses and I think it's nice for the father and the son to have the same after-shaving smell.

I was dressed, too. Although I didn't feel I looked right. This is not how Claude would like to remember me—I looked like I should be at an Easter egg hunt. I didn't look like myself and Daddy didn't smell like himself. If Claude drops by the church as a ghost, he might think he's at the wrong funeral.

I heard Mom coming down the steps. I looked back and saw she was wearing my favorite dress of hers. Sometimes she can be beautiful. When she lets her hair fall natural, she can look as lovely as Jane Pauley, even. Tugging at her waist, Mom said, "I haven't worn this since before Vic. Got it out of the cedar chest. Is it too snug?"

Daddy and me both shook our heads, no. The only problem was there was a strong smell of something that was not quite right. It was mothballs, it was the smell of mothballs and maybe spot remover, too. I shot Daddy a look. From his look, I could tell he had caught the scent. Then I shot Mom a look and she had a look on her face, too. But not from the mothballs, from the Brut—I said nothing. What do you do when you hit a problem like this right before a funeral you're already late for?

In a way, I wish we could have buried Claude in our backyard like we did when my dog Buster got killed in that drive-by.

In our funeral for Buster, we really got it across that we had lost a one-of-a-kind dog— we were not just burying a dead dog—we were saying good-bye to one of the great canine care givers of all time.

In Claude's case, the mistake was in letting the Rotarians run things. It's just, well, here was someone, a true one-of-a-kind, with this great personality who was dead now. And who was in charge of the final send off? These

Rotarians, where you would not find one good personality in the whole bunch.

Claude used to entertain at those luncheons they have. In the funeral service, they made him an "Honorary Rotarian." Daddy said out of the side of his mouth, if he'd wanted to be a member, he would have joined up when he was alive like the others.

I looked down the pew at Grandad and Grandmom. They were holding hands. Even though they were fed up with Claude and his binges most of the time, they loved him all the same. They didn't show it much—it's hard to show love when you feel more fed up with someone than love for them. But still, they love all their sons. Even though they are fed up with all three. Daddy, they're fed up with less, Stanley, now, they're the most fed up with. He has been a real thorn in their sides. And why he came out here from Murfreesboro Correctional. He didn't have to come. He could have used being in prison as a reason not to show up.

Too much for poor Daddy to deal with. One brother's being laid to rest, and one brother brought here from jail by an armed guard. Everyone can see he's wearing one of those electronic alert collars around his big thick ankle.

We were all sitting close together along the pew—there together as a family unit. When I think of all the family feuds, all the name calling, all the critical looks—all through the funeral I could see the critical looks going back and forth—of course the strange scent of moth-balls and after-shave didn't help.

Jack, my cousin, who is sitting at the end of the pew, has been giving me critical looks since we got here. It could be, maybe, that I am at the epicenter of the big Mystery Scent. Who cares? Is all I have to say. Critical looks can't kill you. If they could, there would be one less family unit here at the funeral.

Out of the corner of my eye, at some point, I saw Mom reach over and take Daddy's hand. So I could see Mom and Dad holding hands on the one side, my right, and I looked down at the other end of the pew and could see Grandad and Grandmom still holding hands. They were holding hands to comfort each other. And to see them giving comfort to one another was so comforting to me.

Then, I thought about what Uncle Claude had said, "Remember you're not stuck, Edith, life is about choices." Did he mean I didn't have to be stuck living in Edgetown, stuck in a rut, stuck being with my family?

Knowing Uncle Claude, he meant all of the above. What is being stuck, anyway? It can mean all kinds of things unless—you are stuck with the thought that it means only one thing.

What if you finally do it, you break all your ties with your family to be free, to be yourself. Only what if you don't feel free—you feel alone.

I will always, always, always stick by my family. I will always stick by the people I love. Even if I don't know why I love them. Even if

I can't come up with good reasons why I should stick by them.

This might seem like being stuck to some people, to Claude maybe, but I have the choice. I can choose to see this as not being stuck.

I thought back to what Dr. Lopez said once. I wrote it down—quote—"Love may be hard to understand," she said, "but it is not hard to love. It's so simple. Love is so much easier than we think, what's hard is getting to the place where you see how easy it is." Those were almost her exact words, I'm pretty sure.

Then what popped into my mind was this great book I read about the history of humanity. Next thing I knew I was back in the Dark Ages. I was with a group of cave-types. The same group that had learned to walk upright and to make fire. A man in our crowd had just suddenly keeled over and died. Coronary arrest. A short, squat man of normal height and I.Q. We were used to dead bodies, that's why they called it the Dark Ages. So, we were packing up, about to move on, see, and leave the dead body to the wolves. Then, all of a sudden, someone up front, the leader, stops and turns back, "Wait," she says, "we just can't leave him here like this!"

And then someone says, "Why not? Such is our custom." And a young voice, me, answers, "See that drawing of the buffalo, there on the wall? Well, the dead man did that. I watched him. That's his drawing." "Well, it's not a very good likeness," another voice says, and the leader says, "True, but I watched him, too. I grew to know his face, the blank way he looked when he'd make a mistake—the way his eyes would light up when he captured a certain curve just right." Then other voices were heard:

The way he'd work to erase something he didn't like—

Yeah, he had this goofy way about him. He'd screw up his face and work his tongue to one corner of his lips and then back—

Oh, I remember that about him.

"Yeah, it was like he was drawing along with his tongue."

This made us all smile, for we had all seen this.

"He did not have a natural gift for cave drawing. He had to work so hard—"

"He never gave up until he'd finished."

"But still, it is not a good cave drawing."

"No, the drawing is no good. He was just a nice person."

By the time we'd shared all our memories about this squat, dead caveman, we found we couldn't just leave him there for the wolves. At this point, we had the lightbulb idea to give this man—this average Joe–Six Pack of the Human (Caveman) Species, a proper burial.

Not only out of resepct for him—(I think the book said, but out of respect for ourselves).

After we buried the squat caveman we went back to the cave to celebrate. To mark this historic event. We gathered around the wall with the buffalo drawings. We served deviled dinosaur eggs and Sparkletts mineral water. Then someone said, pointing to the drawing, "Look, at this." We all looked. "This isn't a buffalo, this is an antelope. He'd been drawing an antelope!"

This made us all laugh. Not just at him this time, but at ourselves. So we celebrated ourselves and all of humanity.

And this was the first funeral in the history of humankind. And we thought all our thoughts about the squat caveman out loud and this was the first funeral service and for some reason we were moved to tears. All of us together cried for the first time. And these tears led to the idea that we should give comfort to one another—and this was a moment in history as great—maybe greater even—than the discovery of fire.

At some point I had journeyed back to present time and I picked myself up leaving the church. I had gone through Claude's funeral without one tear or thinking much about

Claude at all. I think all our minds had been wandering. The car doors started opening and we all piled in.

At this point, we all rode out to be together with Grandad and Grandmom at their new mobile home at the Lake Vista Trailer Park where they now have, finally, a 24-hour security guard. I was worried that it might be a problem to get Stanley past the guard with his electronic ankle collar. But the subject never came up.

Just goes to show, some security! I could not believe it, the way they just let a known criminal breeze in—no questions asked. And Stanley, if we'd given him the leeway, was the type who would've stripped the trailer park of all valuables down to the last bingo prize. But I guess, maybe, the ankle collar kept him in line.

Stanley told us about prison life and all. How the food was, violence—stuff I mostly already knew. Then we ate and then we drove all the way down to the lake. Grandad asked us if we'd like to see some of the newer deluxe mobile homes and we acted like we thought it would be a good thing to do.

I'll say this for mobile homes—they get better all the time. You no sooner think you've seen the latest, most deluxe model than they come out with some new dreamhouse improvement, no matter which model you buy, there's always a model that's got some new feature you wish you had. For this reason, I worry that Grandad will never be satisfied living in a trailer park.

We talked some about Claude, but not nearly enough. I believe we are all angry at him that he died. And how he died. It's almost like the dumb stupidity of it is something we just don't want to think about. The Rotarians didn't bring it up either.

Then it came time to leave. We would've stayed longer but we had to pick up Vic on the way back, so we left to go home. And Stanley left to go back to prison. In the car, I saw Daddy staring off into space or maybe back at a memory. He has had a run of bad luck with his brothers. I knew that look. He wanted a drink. I shot a look over at Mom. She knew, too. The three of us shot some looks back and forth to let each other know we knew.

I knew—or felt I knew, he wasn't going to take one—and I shot this signal over to Mom and then to Daddy. I'm pretty sure they got it.

And I am in the back seat now thinking how different the heat from a car heater is from the heat of a hot summer day. I had started out counting the porch lights that were on, but it got too confusing because too many houses already had their Christmas lights up. Some rooftops were already crowded with reindeer and Santas, and some of the Santas were even waving. Amazing!

Wonder what would it be like to be part of that kind of family. The kind to get out all that stuff each year, put it all up, so organized, so filled with holiday spirit and money to burn. Miracle families. These families had a place for everything and everything in its place. My sawdust puppet wouldn't be lost. It would be in a box, wrapped and marked "Sawdust Puppet," safe for all time. Still, I bet, they have their critical looks problems, too. Probably a lot of them as they're putting up those decorations.

This part here, I think I'll skip over because you can picture it yourselves. It was the usual scene of a family coming home, scuffling around some, opening and closing the refrigerator door, a loose magnet fell on Daddy's bare foot. Upstairs, pajamas, bed. It seemed too much like any other night, but I think it may have been just an act. I tossed an ice cube in Hug's water. Hug, she likes it cold.

Before I got to bed, I jotted down a note to Roddy McDowell—I asked for an autographed note to Irene. She *could* come back. I want to give her something nice for Christmas.

I could not finish. It takes a lot of planning and thought to write a celebrity. I fell into bed like a person who maybe had C.F.S. I enter a dream that had already started without me. It was a garage sale. And I saw that someone was buying my sawdust puppet and I cried out, "No, please, I must have that. It's mine!" And

I ran and grabbed it and it just crumbled back into sawdust.

Then this dog ran up to me and I woke up because Hug was trying to wake me up. I heard something and looked out. I saw this shadow move across the porch. It was the shadow of my boney-assed big sister. I could see from her shadow alone that she had lost weight. Her arms flapping, juggling her gear, she took on the form of a Swiss army knife, opening up.

I called down, "Irene, you're back." And she said, "I heard about Claude." And I said, "Be glad you missed the funeral." And then I said, "Vic can walk, now." And I could hear Mom and Dad in the hall, on their way down the steps. I put on my good robe, picked up a few stray items of mine that had leaked over to her side of the room.

And I came into the kitchen and I see my big sister. And she looks thinner. No more body piercing, though, looks like. I thought about saying, "You are a sight for sore eyes," but I didn't. I just went over to be next to them—part of the family unit. Somehow we worked it out so we could be holding on to some part of each other. Irene's skin felt so good, like the cool side of a pillow. And I thought, this could be one of those moments that becomes a moment I will never forget.

It was not the first time we had seen each other cry. And knowing us, it would not be the last time. But it was the first time we were all close like this together. I didn't know exactly how or what to do. But I wanted her to know she had people in her life who wanted to comfort her. And that I was one of them.

Then Irene said, "What's that smell? It's making me nauseous." And we laughed together, where a few minutes before we had been crying. Which is probably how it is going to be for the rest of my life.